"GET LOST, LITTLE BROTHER"

THE STORY OF JOSEPH

By Marilyn Lashbrook

Illustrated by Stephanie McFetridge Britt

D0928426

CANDLE
BOOKS

The story of Joseph is one that every small child can relate to. So often, little ones are rejected by older brothers, sisters and neighbour children. It will encourage your child to know that, in time, he or she will grow up and have a good relationship with siblings. Meanwhile, help your little one feel bigger by teaching him to "read" the capitalized words in the story. After your child becomes familiar with the story, pause when you come to the words printed in capitals and allow your child to fill them in. "GET LOST, LITTLE BROTHER" is a fun way for your child to learn about trusting God and forgiving others.

Copyright © Rainbow Studies International
All rights reserved

First published in the UK in 1992 by Candle Books
(a publishing imprint of Lion Hudson plc).
This edition published in 2007.

Distributed by Marston Book Services Ltd,
PO Box 269, Abingdon, Oxon OX14 4YN

Worldwide co-edition produced by
Lion Hudson plc, Mayfield House,
256 Banbury Road, Oxford OX2 7DH
Tel: +44 (0) 1865 302750
Fax: +44 (0) 1865 302757
Email: coed@lionhudson.com
www.lionhudson.com

ISBN 978 1 85985 700 7

Printed in China

"GET LOST, LITTLE BROTHER"

THE STORY OF JOSEPH

Taken from Genesis 37– 45

Joseph's father gave
him a new coat.
Oooh, it was beautiful.

None of his brothers
had one like it.
They felt LEFT OUT.

Joseph was HAPPY,
but his brothers were ANGRY.

They went outside by themselves.
And they left Joseph behind.

"Go and find your brothers,"
Joseph's father said one day.
So Joseph went to look for them.

Flip, flop, flippity, flap.
His sandals slapped
against the ground.

Joseph looked and looked.
Finally he found his brothers.

But they were still ANGRY.
They did not want to see
"Little Brother" again.

They took away his beautiful coat
and threw him into a deep, dark hole.

Down, down Joseph tumbled.
Thump, thump, bumpity, bump.
"Help! Help!" he cried.
But they would not listen.

"Let's send him away," his brothers said.
"Then he will be gone for good."

Crunch, crunch, crunchity, crunch.
The camels took Joseph away to Egypt.

Joseph was LONELY.
He wanted to go HOME.
But God had a special job for him.

Joseph grew bigger.
And older.
And stronger.
And wiser.

One day, GOD gave Joseph
a message for the king.

"For seven years there will be lots of food. Then for seven years there will be none."

"What should we do?" asked the king.
Without food we will all die!"

Joseph answered,
"We must save all the food we can.
Then there will be plenty
when we need it."

The king was HAPPY.
He made Joseph his special helper.

The king gave him a new robe.
Joseph was very important now.
Everyone in Egypt had to obey him.

Joseph told the people
to fill big barns with grain.

After seven years,
everyone ran out of food.
But Joseph had plenty.

Hungry people with growling
tummies came to Egypt.
Rumble, grumble, gurgle, grrr.
They wanted something to eat.

Even Joseph's brothers came.
Rumble, grumble, gurgle, grrr.
They were hungry, too!

His brothers did not know who Joseph was.
He looked different now.
But Joseph knew them.

"I am Joseph!" he cried.
They were AFRAID,
but Joseph hugged and kissed them all.